STAINED GLASS

PHOTOGRAPHY BY SONIA HALLIDAY AND LAURA LUSHINGTON

*For hundreds of years the makers of stained glass windows
have enriched and beautified cathedrals and churches
right across Europe. This magnificent heritage, a feast of
glorious colour, lives on as an inspiration both to
admirers and craftsmen.*

An ancient art form

The art of making stained glass windows has been practised in England for at least thirteen hundred years. The earliest known reference dates from 675 when Benedict Biscop imported workmen from France to glaze the windows of the monastery of St Peter which he was building at Monkwearmouth in Northumberland. But the use of window glass goes back much further in history. Although vessel glass was made in very early times, window glass seems to have been a Roman invention of the early Imperial period. However, the Romans do not appear to have used translucent coloured glass for windows and this, as well as the invention of lead strips to hold the pieces of glass together, seems to have originated in the Byzantine world. We do not know when these two discoveries, crucial to the making of stained glass windows, took place, but the technique was certainly well established in Europe by 1110–30 when the monk Theophilus, who was probably from Germany, wrote his famous *Diversarium Artium Schedula*. By the 12th century complex techniques of stained glass manufacture had evolved and the essential methods have remained more or less unaltered right to the present day. Theophilus, a 12th-century monk, wrote a description of all the basic processes of making a stained glass window. Coloured glass, known as 'metal', was made by adding various metallic oxides to the crucibles in which the glass was melted. Cobalt gave blue, copper green, iron red and so forth. The molten glass was then blown and shaped into sheets. Natural pot-metal glass coloured blue or red was too dark to transmit much light and so the medieval glazier hit on the technique of applying or 'flashing' a thin layer of the coloured glass on to a sheet of white glass, thus getting over the problem. The detailed design for the window was drawn at full scale on to a whitened flat wooden table, with the areas of the different colours defined, and the panes of white or coloured glass were cut to the

LEFT: 'Leading up' – cutting the grooved malleable lead strips to fit the glass pieces.

BELOW LEFT: Preparing the glass for etching.

BELOW: Glazed in about 1145, this panel in Le Mans Cathedral is one of the earliest examples of French stained glass.

correct shapes to fit into the pattern. This was done by nibbling away at the edge with a notched tool known as a 'grozing iron'. Then these pieces of glass were painted with faces, folds of drapery, inscriptions and so forth. The only pigment used was black; other colour was supplied by the glass itself. We should, in fact, speak of 'stained and painted glass' if we wish to describe the medium accurately. After painting, the panes had to be baked in a small kiln for the short time necessary to flux the black on to the surface of the glass. The panes were then relaid on the table with the design, and the whole bound together with the grooved leaden strips of H section

known as 'calms', which were cut and soldered where necessary. The leads themselves played a very important part in the early windows, for they gave a strong black outline to the design. Windows would be made in panels of convenient size for handling and transport, as they were extremely heavy. The panels would not be joined till they were placed one by one in the window opening. Here they would be held in place by iron 'saddle bars' set in the masonry, to which they were tied by copper wire strips soldered on to the leads. In early windows the iron bars were often bent to follow the curved or angular divisions of the design in the glass.

Bible stories in glass

The earliest English coloured windows, such as those installed in 675 at Monkwearmouth and at the chapel of King Edwin at York shortly afterwards, probably consisted of little more than a simple mosaic. No windows of this type have survived and it is not until the Augsburg cathedral panels and those at St Denis in Paris of the 12th century that we can form any idea of how complete windows must have looked. After St Denis come the great French Gothic churches of Chartres, Notre Dame in Paris, Sens, Noyon and others. Canterbury, which is the only English

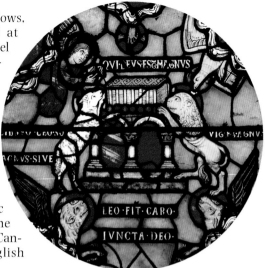

cathedral to contain any considerable quantity of 12th-century stained glass, should be included with these French churches, since the architect chosen to rebuild the choir, destroyed by fire in 1174, was the Frenchman William of Sens. The earliest windows at Canterbury are in the clerestory and were probably completed by 1184. They followed a comprehensive scheme, each window containing two figures, one above the other, representing the lineal descent of Christ from Adam. Like the panels showing Old Testament prophets in the south-west transept, they were designed on a generous scale so that they could be seen clearly from the ground. The painting, accentuated by the lead lines, has great simplicity and strength, with a powerful sense of movement. The colours are deep and very little white glass was used, since too much strong light would destroy the harmony of the darker colours.

At this early date English and French stained glass are closely related. The coloured glass for Canterbury was brought from France as was the stone for the building. Throughout the Middle Ages the English made only clear glass; and we imported our coloured glass, and a good deal of white glass too, either from Normandy or from the Rhineland and Burgundy. But the Canterbury win-

ABOVE: A 12th-century panel in York Minster. The oldest glass in England is at York Minster, and one fragment is believed to date from 1150.

LEFT: Part of the Noah Window in Chartres Cathedral. It dates from about 1210 and shows the luminous blues and rubies which the French so loved.

RIGHT: The early 13th-century St Cecilia Window in St Kunibert's Church, Cologne, shows the yellows and greens which the German glassmakers favoured. The style of the window is completely different from the English and French styles of the same period.

dows were certainly made on the spot and they were designed as a comprehensive scheme. At this early date some of the men involved in designing and making the windows may have been clerics but already, and increasingly as time went on, the glaziers were laymen. During the Middle Ages the more important glaziers' workshops were generally situated in the cathedral towns or places with a concentration of ecclesiastical buildings, since these provided for them a continuing source of work, both for new windows and for repairs.

In the lower windows at Canterbury single large figures would have been out of scale. Although the windows are smaller than in later Gothic churches they are not interrupted by mullions or tracery. In fact the designer had a large space to fill. He followed the example set by Abbot Suger at St Denis, of dividing the space into medallions or panels of different shapes, each containing a scene which formed part of a sequence in a single story.

ABOVE: *A 13th-century roundel in Canterbury Cathedral depicts the siege of the city by the Danes.*

BELOW: *One of the Canterbury panels dating from the 13th century showing the life and miracles of St Thomas à Becket.*

performed after his death. The stories are illustrated with great visual economy, rather in the manner of a strip-cartoon, while the brilliance of the colours and the dramatic intensity of the painting make these windows some of the masterpieces of English stained glass.

The only other important remains of early 13th-century stained glass in England are to be found in Lincoln Minster. These are in the great round window in the north transept where originally there was an entire Day of Judgement

The earliest of the medallion windows at Canterbury, those of about 1200, are the twelve in the north and south choir aisles and the transepts. They are devoted to 'types' and 'anti-types'; that is to say, a scene from the New Testament is associated with one or more from the Old Testament which were thought to have foreshadowed it. These scenes are accompanied by explanations in Latin verse.

The elaborate programme reflected by subjects such as these was systematised in two works, the *Biblia Pauperum* in the early 13th century and in the later *Speculum Humanae Salvationis* (the Mirror of Man's Salvation). They continued to provide subject-matter for stained glass windows for hundreds of years.

Canterbury at this time was a major pilgrimage centre. St Thomas à Becket had been martyred in 1170 and his body was moved from the crypt to a new shrine in the Trinity Chapel in 1220. The windows of the aisles round the chapel were devoted to the life of St Thomas and to the miracles

PASTORALEM DORUMEUA MIPVER EGITE QUORUM

scene. However, a number of other 13th-century panels survive in the Jerusalem Chamber at Westminster as well as in various country churches, for instance at Madley in Herefordshire. Again we find the same range of colours and a similar simplification and boldness of expression.

At this period another type of window was also made using mainly white glass. In 1134 the ascetic Cistercian order had forbidden in its own churches the use of coloured or figured glass. But there were other reasons why

churches outside the order should have relatively plain windows. Not only was it cheaper but it also let in more light. Such glass was mainly white, thinly painted in outline with black foliage patterns. Sometimes spots of coloured glass were added to give variety, as can be seen in the 'Five Sisters' window at York. This type of glass is known as 'grisaille'. The earliest grisaille window in England, at Brabourne in Kent, is of the late 12th century. Here the window space is divided into medallions as with contemporary pictorial glass, but later, as in the 'Five Sisters' window, the whole surface is covered with complicated patterns of weaving foliage.

7

The 14th century and a change of style

Great changes in Gothic architectural style took place between the 13th and 14th centuries, with the transition from the simpler 'Early English' style to the flamboyant 'Decorated' style. Design became richer and freer and most surfaces were covered with a flurry of carved detail. These changes brought difficulties rather than opportunities for the glass designer. Windows became far larger to let in more light and the areas of glass between the vertical stone mullions became immensely long and narrow with small tracery lights at the top. This precluded the use of large figures or complicated jigsaws of medallions, as at Canterbury. The glazier's solution was to place small pictorial panels in bands across the window between areas of grisaille. These pictorial panels were often padded out with architectural canopies over them, as in the 'Pilgrims Window' of the early 14th century and the west window of about 1338, both in York Minster. The figure subjects are subordinated to the general decorative scheme and there is a loss of narrative power. Royal coats of arms or those of the donors of a window are found in the west window of Salisbury Cathedral as early as the third quarter of the 13th century but now become more common. Sometimes figures of the donors themselves appear, as in the Henry de Mamesfield window (c.1300) at Merton College, Oxford, where the

FAR RIGHT: A window at All Saints, Eaton Bishop, a superb example of early 14th-century English stained glass.

RIGHT: A detail from the window at Eaton Bishop. The yellow was made by firing a derivative of sulphide of silver onto the surface of the glass.

BELOW: The Henry de Mamesfield window (c.1300) at Merton College, Oxford.

<8></8>

kneeling figures of the donor have backgrounds of damask patterns with, above and below, areas of complex grisaille ornament, leaded up in elaborate designs and relieved with small pieces of coloured glass and single heads. More often grisaille painting is found on diamond-shaped panes known as 'quarries'. Both quarries and textural backgrounds become increasingly common.

Some idea of the changes in style that took place in English stained glass in the early 14th century can be seen in the panel of the Virgin and Child from Eaton Bishop in Herefordshire. A softness and sweetness appear in faces and the figures have a graceful sway, characteristics which have as their background the humanism we associate with the teaching of St Francis.

Besides these changes of mood there were also important technical developments. About the beginning of the century it was discovered that white glass could be stained a yellow colour, ranging from a pale lemon to a deep orange, by firing on to the surface a derivative of sulphide of silver. This meant that a golden halo, for example, could be painted on to the same piece of glass as the head where previously a separate piece of glass would have been leaded

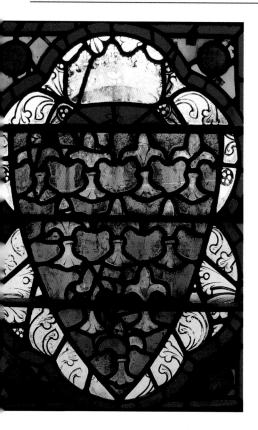

on. The advantages are particularly clear in the panel of the Virgin and Child, where yellow stain can be seen on the hair, crown and bird. Besides silver stain some new colours begin to be used, particularly brown, violet and deep green. Painting has become more sophisticated, with stippling taking the place of the earlier type of smearing or scratching through a wash of black enamel pigment. Foliage is also becoming more naturalistic and architectural canopies are rendered with perspective. Borders become increasingly standardised, frequently consisting of repeated motifs often borrowed from heraldry.

York Minster has the largest group of windows of this period but magnificent glass is also to be found elsewhere. Some of the most beautiful is in the north aisle of the choir at Wells Cathedral, where a figure (c.1320–25) of St Michael fighting a dragon is a particularly fine example. Like the St Michael

from Eaton Bishop, this figure has a gentle charm and graceful sway of the body. In contrast with earlier glass all drama has disappeared, and the dragon is rather more suggestive of a tiresome lapdog than a fearsome adversary. The glass has a characteristic lightness and brilliance that is far removed from the depth of colour found in the early windows at Canterbury. The panels of about 1340 in the tracery of the Becket window in St Lucy's Chapel, Oxford Cathedral, admirably illustrate the changes which have taken place by the mid-14th century. The elaborate stonework is filled with heraldic devices, kneeling figures (who may be donors), monsters such as are commonly found in the illuminated manuscripts of the period, and figures and scenes set on a rich background of ornament. The total effect is one of great sophistication, a quality found in the Virgin and Child at Eaton Bishop, as well as of strength and a subtlety of colour. However, the Virgin and Child at Fladbury in Worcestershire is an example of a far more primitive type of glass still to be found in the first half of the 14th century. It possesses a strangeness of proportion and strength of drawing which saves it from the near-sentimentality of figures like the St Catherine from Deerhurst in Gloucestershire.

The colours and style of the glass of this period did not survive unchanged for long, although they are still present, for example, in the seven windows of the clerestory of the choir at Tewkesbury Abbey (c.1340–44). From the middle of the century onwards, with the development of 'Perpendicular' tracery, more and more white glass was used both for canopies and for the robes and faces of figures. As we have seen, grisaille had earlier been used for deliberately lightening the effect of a window, but nothing had yet been done which can be compared with the best example of this tendency, the great east window of Gloucester Cathedral, erected in 1350–60, perhaps in memory of the

LEFT: The arms of Louis IX of France, in Salisbury Cathedral, date from the late 13th century. Although used quite widely on the continent at that time, it was not until the early 14th century that coats of arms were seen more frequently in England.

RIGHT: Tewkesbury Abbey in Gloucestershire. These knights, dressed in the armour of the period (c.1340–44), are good examples of stained glass portraiture. Such portraits were not meant to be authentic likenesses; identification depended mainly on costume and inscriptions.

The growing importance of the glazier

RIGHT: *A 14th-century German panel in the Münster Landesmuseum features a knight at prayer. He would have commissioned the portrait of himself and paid for the window. Donor windows became increasingly popular throughout Europe at this time.*

FAR RIGHT: *The 14th-century window in the Lady Chapel of Wells Cathedral shows the elaborate tracery of the time and how the glaziers filled the space available to them.*

BELOW: *The monkey's funeral forms the border of a 14th-century window in York Minster.*

battle of Crécy. The general impression is of red and blue, in a great expanse of white. The drawing is somewhat harsh and very little yellow is used. In marked contrast is the glass from William of Wykeham's twin foundations of Winchester and New College, Oxford. The ante-chapel at New College still possesses a magnificent series of figures painted in soft, subtle colours, while three prophets from Winchester College, the sole remaining complete figures from the side walls of the chapel, are now to be found in the Victoria and Albert Museum in London. They are portrayed in elaborate architectural niches against backgrounds of rich scrolling foliage. Both chapels originally possessed large representations of the 'Tree of Jesse', illustrating the descent of Christ from Jesse, a subject popular in England throughout the Middle Ages.

The glass at both these foundations was executed by a glazier named Thomas of Oxford. He and his assistants painted the New College glass in 1380–83 and that at Winchester from *c.*1393–1404. These commissions are unusual in that the name of the artist is known. By the late 14th century the glazier was improving his position in society and it is perhaps significant in this context that Thomas of Oxford

included a self-portrait at the base of the Winchester College Jesse Tree. With the increase in the size of windows there was a corresponding growth in the number of glaziers at work. We know the names of only a dozen or so stained glass artists before 1250 but thirty-two have been found recorded between the years 1250 and 1300. Many more must have existed but these figures give some idea of the proportional growth of numbers. It is also interesting to note that during the 14th century the centres of stained glass production became more numerous. Workshops existed in such places as Bath, Canterbury, Chester, Chichester, Exeter, Gloucester, King's Lynn, Lewes, Lincoln, Norwich, Oxford, Southwark, Westminster and York, as well as in quite small villages. By the 15th century local differences in style can be detected even within a particular region such as the West Country. By 1364–65 the glaziers were sufficiently well established to petition to set up their own guild. Symptomatic of this rise in status was the institution of the post of King's Glazier and we know that in 1393, in the reign of Richard II, George Savage was appointed for life. The position may have existed earlier but from this period onwards it became a regular appointment.

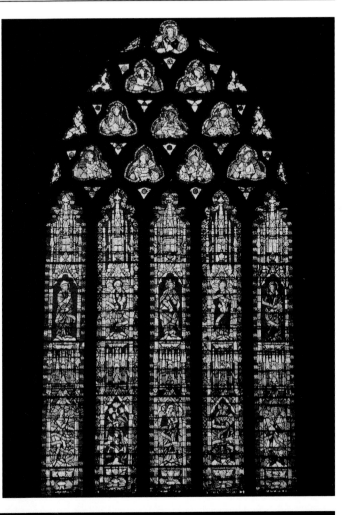

In certain respects the glass at Winchester and New College anticipated the commonest form of 15th-century window, the use of tiers of figures under tall elaborate canopies. The glass appears more transparent owing to the use of more white glass and fewer, paler colours. Borders become narrower, there is less interest in pattern and more in brush-work and drawing. Narrative acquires a great importance and subject-matter becomes far more varied. This richness of subject-matter is particularly evident at Great Malvern Priory, which has more glass of the first half of the 15th century than any other building in England. The great east window at York Minster, carried out by John Thornton of Coventry between 1405 and 1408, demonstrates this tendency towards narrative with its row upon row of little rectangular pictures crowded with figures. The scenes are delightful and beautifully drawn, although they are in many ways unsuitable for the great height at which many of them are placed. Small panels of this kind can be much better appreciated in the small parish churches of York, such as All Saints, North Street, or in the Norfolk churches such as East Harling, North Tuddenham or St Peter Mancroft in Norwich.

The 15th century also saw the rise

of stained glass intended purely for domestic settings. Roundels of the 'Labours of the Months', for example, became popular, as did quarries (square- or diamond-shaped panes of glass) painted with subjects such as the amusing little birds now in Yarnton church, Oxfordshire, which seem to have come from a secular setting. The growing use of stained glass in secular settings is reflected in churches by the greater prominence given to donor figures, as can be seen at Long Melford in Suffolk and at St Neot in Cornwall (c.1480–1530). Heraldry was also much used, normally in the tracery lights of churches.

TOP LEFT: Noah digging in his vineyard. One of the wide variety of subjects to be found in Great Malvern Priory.

LEFT: A scene from the east window of St Peter Mancroft.

TOP RIGHT: The month of February from the 'Labours of the Months' at Brandiston Hall in Norfolk.

RIGHT: A 15th-century quarry (a diamond-shaped panel of glass) which was originally in an inn and is now in St Bartholomew's Church, Yarnton.

ABOVE: *A 15th-century panel in Long Melford, Suffolk.*

OPPOSITE: *The Jesse Window at St Margaret's, Margaretting, probably made by John Prudde, King's Glazier in the reign of Henry VI.*

to more ordinary glass by Prudde for which he charged one shilling and two pence. The sumptuous effect of the glass was enhanced by the use of contrasting glass 'jewels' which were inserted into holes drilled in the glass of the robes. Stained glass almost as brilliant as that in the Beauchamp Chapel is to be found at Browne's Hospital, Stamford, but was made much later – about 1485.

Another window which can probably be associated with Prudde is the Jesse Tree at Margaretting church in Essex (*c.*1460). For the artist this subject had the advantage that the branches and tendrils rising from the recumbent form of Jesse and which enclose the figures of his descendants could be used to carry the design across the mullions of the window. As windows became larger the problem of how to escape the limitations imposed by the architectural framework became more acute. A less satisfactory solution can be seen in the Canterbury window (*c.*1482) showing Edward IV with his wife Elizabeth Woodville and their children; here the figures are linked visually by a background of similar curtains. The logical answer was to ignore the mullions altogether and to treat the window as an unbroken pictorial space, as was already being done on the Continent. This tendency can be seen in the 'Magnificat' window of 1501 at Great Malvern. But the best examples of this period are the windows at Fairford in Gloucestershire carried out between 1495 and 1505. Here the Crucifixion takes up the whole of the east window and the Last Judgment the whole of the west. Although their appearance is truly splendid the painting departs from the 15th-century tradition both in detail and in general pictorial character, looking distinctly unEnglish. This is not surprising since we know that there was a considerable influx of foreign artists, amongst them glass-painters, at this time. Foreign glaziers had been at work in England for some time but they had had little effect. Now foreign influence was

Some of the richest 15th-century windows are those made by John Prudde, King's Glazier in the reign of Henry VI, for the Beauchamp Chapel in St Mary's, Warwick, in about 1447–50. These have a luxurious depth of colour and delicacy of painting giving the impression that no expense was too great to provide a suitable memorial to Richard Beauchamp, Earl of Warwick. This was even literally true as the windows cost two shillings a square foot as opposed

markedly stronger, as can be seen in the draughtsmanship of the early 16th century sequence showing the miracles of St Nicholas, at All Saints, Hillesden, Buckinghamshire.

Although the foreigners were not popular, they were patronised by the court. From 1496 onwards Henry VII employed Barnard Flower who was either a Fleming or a German. In or before 1505 Flower became King's Glazier and from 1515 until his death in 1517 he worked on the windows of the newly completed King's College Chapel in Cambridge. Flower was succeeded both at King's College and as the King's Glazier by Galyon Hone, who was probably a Fleming. In 1526 two contracts were made for continuing the glazing of King's College Chapel with Hone and five other glaziers, most of them foreigners.

The huge east window at King's well illustrates the problem facing glaziers of the period and the solution they worked out. They divided the window in half horizontally, taking the subjects right across the window and ignoring the mullions. The lower part of each scene was filled with figures, the upper part was given sky and architecture. The solution is far from happy and is even less satisfactory in the side windows where the discrepancy between the height and width is too great, posing insoluble problems for the designer. The drawing, however, is extremely fine. Here, and to a lesser degree in the glass of such places as Temple Guiting in Gloucestershire, the northern Renaissance is amply in evidence. But it is worth remembering that plenty of English glaziers were at work in the first half of the 16th century on whom this alien style had little or no effect. This can be seen, for example, in the Jesse Tree of 1533 at Dyserth in Flintshire.

LEFT: Fairford, Gloucestershire. 'The Last Judgement', the work of Flemish glaziers between 1495 and 1505. Their work brought a greater degree of realism to stained glass.

BELOW: A detail from the bottom right hand corner of 'The Last Judgement' – the Jaws of Hell.

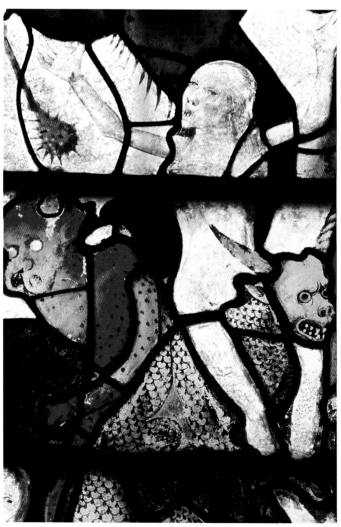

ABOVE: *A 15th-century panel in Ulm Minster in Germany by Hans Acker, showing the dove returning to Noah in the ark. Panels such as these influenced stained-glass makers in England.*

ABOVE: *A late 16th-century French enamel painted panel in the Rouen Museum gives a vivid impression of the interior of a rich household.*

OPPOSITE: *Foreign influence can again be seen in this panel of the miracles of St Nicholas in All Saints, Hillesden.*

At just the moment when the Renaissance was beginning to have an effect on the appearance of stained glass, politics intervened. Henry VIII's wish to divorce Catherine of Aragon and to marry Anne Boleyn led eventually to the 'Reformation Parliament' of 1529–36 and the iconoclasm that followed. In some ways the Reformation came in the nick of time. By the second half of the 16th century the art of stained glass had reached a crisis. Designs were provided by specialists who thought and cared more about imitating the manner of an appropriate panel painting or fresco than about the technique of the firing and the making up of the stained glass. By this time, architects were building windows whose

size and shape imposed an impossible strain on the stained glass medium. In France and Flanders reasonably successful attempts were made to reconcile these conflicting tendencies. But in England the King's College windows represent the end of the medieval tradition and less than five years after they had been completed, the Reformation was an established fact.

In the first and second Injunctions of Henry VIII of 1536 and 1538, giving instructions regarding churches and other religious buildings, there is no reference to stained glass at all. But part of Article 28 of the 1547 Injunctions of Edward VI reads: 'Also, that they shall take away, utterly extinct and destroy all shrines, coverings of shrines, all tables, candlesticks, trindles or rolls of wax, pictures, paintings, and all other monuments of feigned miracles, pilgrimages, idolatry, and superstition; so that there remain no memory of the same in walls, glass windows, or elsewhere within their churches or houses. And they shall exhort all their parishioners to do the like within their several houses.'

In some churches the glass was destroyed and replaced with clear glass; in others the windows were taken out and hidden or kept for possible reinstatement or for use in repairs. In yet other churches the glass was merely smashed. Where windows were not replaced there was a real danger of the decay of the fabric or furnishings. As a result of this the official policy changed and the Royal Injunctions of 1559 decree the 'preserving nevertheless or repairing the walls and glass windows.' The tide of destruction began to ebb but for many years afterwards windows continued to be broken or allowed to decay and stained glass replaced by white. William Harrison, writing in his *Description of England* in 1577, describes the position:

'Churches themselves, belles and times of morning & evening praier remain as in time past, saving that all images, shrines, tabernacles, rood loftes & monuments of idolatrie are removed, taken down & defaced: Onlie the stories in glasse windowes excepted, which, for want of sufficient store of new stuffe, & by reason of extreame charge that should grow by the alteration of the same into white panes throughoute the realme, are not altogether abolished in most places at once, but by little and little suffered to decaie that white glass may be set up in their rooms.'

The removal of religious subject matter from the repertoire of stained glass artists had a serious effect on the craft. The glaziers' energies had now to be channelled into acceptable subject-matter and virtually all that remained

was heraldry or the 'branches, flowers or posies taken out of Holy Scripture' recommended by Bishop Hooper in his *Injunctions for Gloucester and Worcester* of 1551–52. As a result enormous numbers of heraldic panels were painted at this time. Between 1550 and 1600 at least thirty dated examples are known and many others which are undated survive, although they represent only a fraction of what was made during this period. An example of how this hitherto comparatively unimportant aspect of stained glass painting was raised to an art can be seen in a series of panels by Bernard Dininckhoff painted for Gilling Castle, Yorkshire (*c*.1585). Not only is the armorial painting of great delicacy but the plain quarries form the most delightful and subtle patterns. These panels are interesting for an additional reason. Besides containing pot-metal glass, they are painted in part with enamel colours. In the middle of the 16th century, probably in the Netherlands, it was discovered that glass could be painted with enamel colours made by grinding up coloured glass, mixing it with a suitable vehicle, washing it onto the glass and then firing it in a

muffle kiln of the type that had always been used for fixing the black pigment. This revolution removed the necessity of cutting out the shapes from sheets of pot-metal glass. Instead, the enamel colours could be painted directly on to clear glass, rather in the way that oil colours are applied to a canvas. This meant that the clear glass could be of regular shapes and increasingly it became normal to use rectangular panes. Leading became purely utilitarian and no longer served the artistic purpose of accentuating the painted lines.

The 17th century and Civil War

RIGHT: *A detail from a window in Oxford (see inside front cover), painted by Abraham van Linge in about 1635.*

BELOW: The Adam and Eve window in University College Chapel, Oxford, was painted by Abraham van Linge in 1641.

Although a wide range of enamel colours had not been evolved until the mid-16th century, a red enamel colour had been in use for some time. Enamel pigment can be found for example in some of the King's College windows, used side by side with traditional techniques. If these enamel colours had not been in existence by the early 17th century the glaziers would have been in parlous straits, for in 1636 the main source for the supply of coloured glass was cut off. The war between Louis XIII of France and Duke Charles IV of Lorraine led in 1633 to the destruction of the Lorraine glass-houses. At this time England was almost entirely dependent on this source for pot-metal glass and as a result supplies became virtually non-existent. For the better part of two hundred years pot-metal glass was hardly used in England although efforts were made from time to time to revive its manufacture.

Throughout the 17th century the staple product of the average glazier's shop was heraldic work, as it had been since 1550, but in the second decade there was a significant revival of religious pictorial glass-painting, actively encouraged by William Laud, the Archbishop of Canterbury. The main names associated with this revival are those of the brothers Bernard and Abraham van Linge, members of a glass-painting family of Emden in Friesia. Most of their work is to be found in London and in the Oxford colleges, as well as in Christ Church Cathedral, but it can also be seen at Lydiard Tregoze in Wiltshire. A few other contemporary glass-painters are known, such as Robert Rudland,

Richard Greenbury and Baptista Sutton. Indeed by 1638 there was sufficient activity in the field to encourage the London glaziers' guild to petition successfully to become a City Company.

This revival was short-lived for the Civil War began in 1642. The following year an attack on 'idolatry' was launched and there was a renewed outbreak of iconoclasm. One of the most zealous in this work was William Dowsing, who was appointed Parliamentary Visitor in that year. His diary of his progress through Suffolk is a dreadful catalogue of destruction. In Kent, Richard ('Blue Dick') Culmer, rector of Chartham, tried to break as much glass as possible at Canterbury, taking a pike in his hand, standing on a tall ladder 'ratling down proud Becket's glassy bones'. The Cromwellian armies, too, did considerable damage. 'Lord, what work was here! What clattering of glasses! What beating down of walls! What tearing up of monuments!' In many places the iconoclasm was more

ABOVE: Typical 17th-century glass-painting from the Netherlands, in Bishopsbourne Church, Kent.

LEFT: A sundial at University College, Oxford, designed by Henry Gyles of York, a well-known stained glass maker of the late 17th century. He taught the Price brothers, William and Joshua, who were important makers in the 18th century.

half-hearted. Some merely removed or defaced heads. Others took down complete windows and kept them put away. Although the enthusiasm for such destruction abated gradually it was not until the end of the Commonwealth in 1660 that stained glass was produced again on any scale.

The most important figure of the latter part of the 17th century was Henry Gyles of York (1645–1709). His speciality was heraldic work, which he executed with great delicacy and elaboration as in the arms of Charles II done for Acomb near York in 1663. He used enamel pigments with great subtlety but produced very few pictorial windows. It was not until the 18th century that this branch of the art was revived in the work of two important brothers, William and Joshua Price (who had both been pupils of Henry Gyles), and in that of William's son.

Stability and a fresh start

William Price the elder and his son William are represented in some of the Oxford colleges. But the most impressive examples of the family's work are the ten windows executed by Joshua Price, the younger brother of William Price the elder, in the church at Great Witley, Worcestershire.

Apart from the Price family the most outstanding stained glass painter of the 18th century was William Peckitt, also of York. He was deeply interested in technique, experimenting with colours in an effort to rediscover the secret of making pot-metal glass, and he is said to

LEFT: *Detail from a window in Middleton Cheney, by William Morris and Company.*

BELOW LEFT: *King Solomon in a York Minster window glazed by William Peckitt, one of the outstanding glass-painters of the 18th century.*

have made a successful 'flashed' ruby glass. It is a notable characteristic of 18th-century glass-painters that they emulated easel-painters. Indeed their working methods were in many ways similar and they frequently used cartoons supplied by painters in oils.

Towards the end of the 18th and in the early years of the 19th century there was a growing interest in medieval stained glass. The Gothic Revival entered a more 'correct' and archaeological phase in architecture and the decorative arts. It must be remembered that at this time little knowledge was available on the history of medieval glasspainting or its techniques. Although the 18th-century type of pictorial window continued to be made at least as late as 1854, when Hedgeland of London supplied the west window of Norwich Cathedral, there was also a growing movement towards producing glass in

a more academic medieval style. Pioneer studies on the history of medieval glass became available and manufacturers began to analyse the chemical constituents of medieval glass and once again to produce pot-metal glass of a similar type. Restoration of ancient glass, such as that carried out by Betton and Evans of Shrewsbury for Winchester College, provided a great deal of valuable information on medieval painting and leading techniques.

The most important departure from this new tradition, in stained glass as in other decorative arts, was the firm of Morris and Company, founded by William Morris in 1861. His great contribution was to break away from the cold and over-precise imitation of medieval glass painting of his immediate predecessors and to develop a freer, more flowing style using strong, glowing colours. Morris was fortunate and far-

sighted in being able to call on the services of such artists as Rossetti, Madox Brown and above all Burne-Jones who, like Morris, understood the essential principles of how to use leading and the shape of a window to full effect.

The work of Morris and Company had a liberating influence which inspired a new generation of Arts and Crafts artists in the latter part of the 19th and the early 20th century. Men such as Lethaby, Reynolds-Stephens and Whall all reacted against high Victorian taste to produce original work, much of which, in colouring and the sinuous lines of the drawing, can be legitimately described as Art Nouveau in feeling. Links with the more conventional 19th-century tradition of glass-painting continued in the work of Henry Holiday and others but the stage was

ABOVE: Detail from the St Francis Window of 1924 in Selborne Church, a memorial to Gilbert White, vicar and well-known amateur naturalist.

LEFT: Burne-Jones designed the St Frideswide window in Christ Church, Oxford, in 1858.

New challenges in the 20th century

emerged. The work of Erwin Bossanyi at Canterbury and Evie Hone at Eton College Chapel owes much to the modern movement in painting and has produced strikingly individual solutions to the problem of working in medieval architectural settings. The great changes brought by modern architecture have also produced new challenges; in 1962, in Coventry Cathedral, a group of artists including Lawrence Lee, Keith New, Geoffrey Clark, Patrick Reyntiens and John Piper produced a series of windows with little dependence on realism. Form and colour were manipulated for symbolic purposes and the resulting glass matched the modern spirit of the new cathedral itself.

Such developments have led to a renewed interest in stained glass; and the increased use of panels of coloured glass as a feature of secular buildings points to a new and wider role for the art in England and around the world.

set for the greater degree of experiment so characteristic of the 20th century. In more recent years representational painting has been strongly upheld by A.K. Nicholson, Douglas Strachan, Christopher Webb, Martin Travers, F.C. Eden, Leonard Walker, Reginald Bell, Hugh Easton and Sir Ninian Comper, to take some of the more outstanding names. These artists have little in common, except perhaps a tendency to use more white glass, letting in more light.

At the same time a more abstract and less representational style has also

ABOVE: A detail of the 'Battle of Britain' window in Westminster Abbey, made in 1947 by Hugh Easton.

RIGHT: A window in the cathedral at Chelmsford, designed by Henry Holiday in 1905.